Let's look at
Life below the City

Created by
Claude Delafosse
and Gallimard Jeunesse
Illustrated by Ute Fuhr
and Raoul Sautai

*At the back of this book
you will find a press-out paper torch,
and a pocket to keep it in.*

FIRST DISCOVERY / TORCHLIGHT
MOONLIGHT PUBLISHING

Below a city, it's dark and it's not easy to see. That's a pity because there is so much going on.

In this book you will be able to see everything down below, just as if you were on a guided tour.

Thanks to a simple torch made of paper, you can explore the dark pages of this book.
It's like magic!

You'll find the torch on the last page.
Press it out and slide it between the plastic page
and the black page underneath it.
You'll be amazed at what you "light up"!

Below the house, a cellar!

Under a house, you often find a room
with no windows: it's a cellar.
It is used for storing all kinds of bulky
things, which are seldom used, and also
wine, which keeps better in thee dark

As you move it around, little by little you'll discover all
the details hidden in each picture.

What goes on under the city

When you walk around a city, you see buildings, streets and statues. There are also a lot of things you can't see, because they are below the streets. To discover what is hidden down there, take your magic torch and you will find you can see everything quite clearly.

Below the house, a cellar

Under a house you often find a room
with no windows: it's a cellar.
It is used for storing all kinds of bulky
things, which are seldom used, and also
wine, which keeps better in the dark.
Cellars are favourite places for
mice and spiders.

Below the pavements, pipes!

Often you see workmen digging up
streets with a mechanical drill.
It's because they are laying or repairing
the water or gas pipes or the cables
for electricity or the telephone.

Below the roads, the sewers

Do you know where the water goes,
after you have washed your hands?
It drains into a sewer, a man-made
underground river, which follows
the layout of the city, and takes dirty
water to the waterworks to be purified.

Below the traffic, the tube!

In some big cities, people are able to move around easily underground, thanks to a funny kind of train, known as the tube. It's quicker than travelling by car, because there aren't any traffic jams down there.

Below the streets, car parks!

There are too many cars in our cities and
not enough parking spaces.
So now more and more underground
multi-storey car parks are being built.
You take a ticket as you drive in
and you pay on the way out.

Under the square, the old city!

Sometimes, when they are digging to lay new foundations,
builders come across ancient remains of the city.
Archeologists are called in to excavate the site,
so that we find out how the city used to be.

Below the sea, a train!

in order for trains to cross the English Channel,
engineers built a very long tunnel,
which joined Britain to France.
Eurostar carries train passengers, and
Eurotunnel takes cars and lorries on freight trains.

Sometimes, when a new building is being planned, it is designed to have an underground shopping centre.

This big city telephone company has its computer room, staff lounge and canteen all underground.

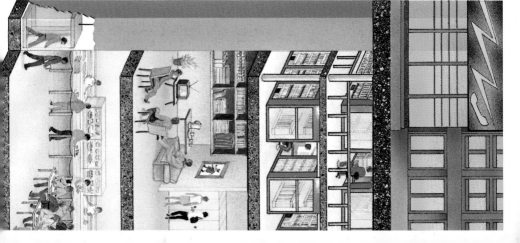

Can you find them using your magic torch?

FIRST DISCOVERY: OVER 100 TITLES AVAILABLE IN FIVE SERIES

AMERICAN INDIANS
ANIMAL CAMOUFLAGE
ANIMALS IN DANGER
BABIES
BEARS
THE BEAVER
THE BEE
BEING BORN
BIRDS
BOATS
THE BODY
THE BUILDING SITE
THE BUTTERFLY
THE CASTLE
CATHEDRALS
CATS
CHRISTMAS AND NEW YEAR
CLOTHES AND COSTUMES
COLOURS
COUNTING
THE CROCODILE
THE DESERT
DINOSAURS
DOGS
DUCKS
THE EAGLE
EARTH AND SKY
THE EGG
THE ELEPHANT
FARM ANIMALS
FINDING A MATE
FIREFIGHTING
FLOWERS
FLYING
FOOTBALL
THE FROG
FRUIT
GROWING UP
HALLOWEEN
HANDS, FEET AND PAWS

HOMES
THE HORSE
HOW THE BODY WORKS
THE INTERNET
THE JUNGLE
THE LADYBIRD
LIGHT
THE LION
MONKEYS AND APES
MOUNTAINS
THE MOUSE
MUSIC
ON WHEELS
THE OWL
PENGUINS
PICTURES
PREHISTORIC PEOPLE
PYRAMIDS
RABBITS
THE RIVERBANK
THE SEASHORE
SHAPES
SHOPS
SMALL ANIMALS IN THE HOME
SPORT
THE STORY OF BREAD
THE TELEPHONE
TIME
THE TOOLBOX
TOWN
TRAINS
THE TREE
UNDER THE GROUND
UP AND DOWN
VEGETABLES
WATER
THE WEATHER
WHALES
THE WIND
THE WOLF

FIRST DISCOVERY / ATLAS

ANIMAL ATLAS
ATLAS OF ANIMALS IN DANGER
ATLAS OF CIVILIZATIONS
ATLAS OF COUNTRIES
ATLAS OF THE EARTH
ATLAS OF FRANCE
ATLAS OF ISLANDS
ATLAS OF PEOPLES
ATLAS OF SPACE
PLANT ATLAS

FIRST DISCOVERY / ART

ANIMALS
HENRI MATISSE
THE IMPRESSIONISTS
LANDSCAPES
THE LOUVRE
PABLO PICASSO
PAINTINGS
PORTRAITS
SCULPTURE
VINCENT VAN GOGH

FIRST DISCOVERY / TORCHLIGHT

LET'S LOOK AT ANIMALS BY NIGHT
LET'S LOOK AT ANIMALS UNDERGROUND
LET'S LOOK AT ARCHIMBOLDO'S PORTRAITS
LET'S LOOK AT CASTLES
LET'S LOOK AT CAVES
LET'S LOOK AT DINOSAURS
LET'S LOOK AT FISH UNDERWATER
LET'S LOOK AT LIFE BELOW THE CITY
LET'S LOOK AT INSECTS
LET'S LOOK AT THE JUNGLE
LET'S LOOK AT THE SKY
LET'S LOOK AT THE ZOO BY NIGHT
LET'S LOOK FOR LOST TREASURE
LET'S LOOK INSIDE THE BODY
LET'S LOOK INSIDE PYRAMIDS

FIRST DISCOVERY CLOSE-UPS

LET'S LOOK AT THE GARDEN CLOSE UP
LET'S LOOK AT THE HEDGE CLOSE UP
LET'S LOOK AT THE POND CLOSE UP
LET'S LOOK AT THE SEASHORE CLOSE UP

Translator: Penelope Stanley-Baker
ISBN 1 85103 313 0
© 1997 by Editions Gallimard Jeunesse

English text © 2001 by Moonlight Publishing Ltd
First published in the United Kingdom 2001
by Moonlight Publishing Limited, The King's Manor, East Hendred, Oxon. OX12 8JY
Printed in Italy by Editoriale Lloyd

The drinking water for a city is tested several times each day in the water purification centre.

Mushrooms are often grown in cities in huge underground cellars.

These details are from the dark pages of the book.

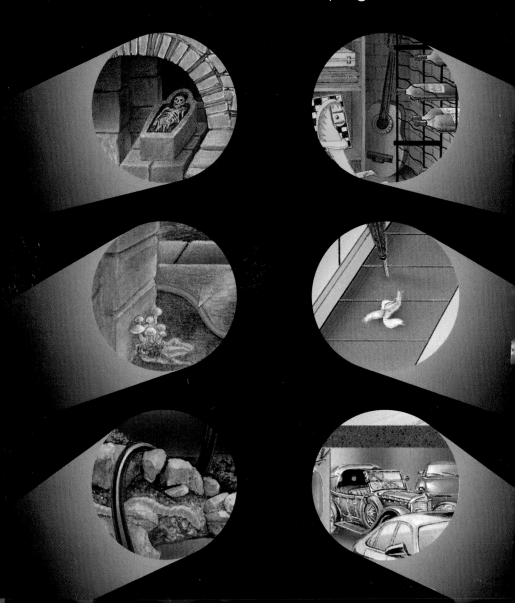